STRANGERS IN THE NIGHT

MY SECRET WEEKEND WITH FRANK SINATRA

Sandra White

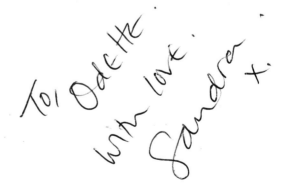

To Odette
with love.
Sandra x.

ISBN: 978-1-326-28997-3

PublishNation, London
www.publishnation.co.uk

For my three children

In the late 80's the Sunday Mirror sent me to spend the weekend with Frank Sinatra. His wife, Barbara Marx, was organising a Magic Carpet Weekend to raise funds for her children's charity. The Sunday Mirror bought two tickets. They cost £14,000, an incredible amount of money for the paper to spend back then. Today that would be more than £32,000.

The subsequent article launched the Sunday Mirror's colour supplement and my weekend with Frank became my claim to fame. Even now people will introduce me as the woman who spent the weekend with Frank Sinatra.

I have never disclosed what really happened that weekend. STRANGERS IN THE NIGHT: MY SECRET WEEKEND WITH FRANK SINATRA reveals everything. 2015 seems the right time to tell the whole story – Ol' Blue Eyes would have been 100 on December 12.

ONE

It was a bizarre instruction: the editor's secretary ringing me to tell me to go to see the features editor immediately. The features editor wasn't my boss. I had nothing to do with him. I was a news reporter on the Sunday Mirror, one of Britain's biggest selling tabloids and I answered to the news editor.

The features editor's office was one of several glass boxes at the end of the long open plan office. As I made my way past the news desk I looked at my boss to see if he would give me a clue. He kept his head down. "He knows something," I thought. The Sunday Mirror had a small staff compared to other Sunday tabloids, we were always under immense pressure. I was up to my eyes in stories for that week's paper, one of which was potentially the splash, the front page story. I couldn't see my boss agreeing to me helping out the features department.

I knocked on the glass door. Peter Miller, assistant editor (features), number three on the paper after the editor and deputy editor, was leaning back in his chair, grinning. I sat the other side of his desk as he explained that a stringer, a freelance journalist, in LA had discovered that Barbara Sinatra was organising a fund raising weekend for her children's charity. For $25,000 you could join Frank and Barbara Sinatra on a Magic Carpet Weekend, meeting the Sinatra's at their home and flying to Las Vegas with them and their guests. It sounded interesting but I still didn't get what this had to do with me.

"We have bought two tickets," Peter said casually. $25,000? That was a vast amount of money for the Sunday Mirror to shell out. Our newspaper was almost always out bid by rival newspapers on 'buy-ups,' exclusive interviews. The most I had ever known us spend was £10,000. I quickly reckoned $25,000 was about £14,000.

"Wow!" I was impressed.

Peter brought his chair forward. "Yeah. The editor wants you to go."

"Me?" I looked through the glass wall to the feature writers.

Peter knew what I was thinking, why wasn't someone in his own department going?

"But…"

Peter interrupted me: "We want you to go. The editor wants you to go," he repeated, "there is just one stumbling block."

"Yes…"

"Sinatra hates journalists so they won't let you in. You will have to go undercover. They will think you are a wealthy married couple. You will have to act the part and, of course, you will have to share a room with the stringer, Ian Black. I am sure he will be a gentleman and sleep on the sofa." Peter laughed.

"Go undercover?" I repeated, "pretend we're married?"

"It will be sensational. Frank Sinatra has not given any interviews for years. No-one knows anything about him any more. You will get to know him and be able to write about the real Frank Sinatra, the man behind the legend. Get behind the hype and the myth." He was talking in headlines.

"This is a massive amount of money for us to spend. The editor needs someone who can hold their nerve, someone she trusts to turn in the goods, she wants you to go. We all agree you are the right one for the job.

"It will be a top secret operation. No-one must know. You can't tell anyone out there," he nodded towards the newsroom. "Will you do it?"

Without hesitation I replied: "Yes."

I wandered back to my desk. As I passed the news desk I looked at my boss. He smiled and called me into his office. "Did you say yes?" he asked.

"Yes."

"Great. You will do a fantastic job. Just goes to show they haven't got anyone in features up to it!"

Back at my desk I stared at the blank page on my notebook and tried to take in what had just happened. I am going to spend the weekend with Frank Sinatra. Frank Sinatra! One of the most famous men in the world. Legend. Francis Albert! Ol' Blue Eyes. Wow! I wanted to shout out: "I'm going to spend the weekend with Frank Sinatra." But I couldn't tell anyone!

There were three people at home I could tell: my two children and our nanny, Julia. The children, aged 11 and nine, hardly knew who Frank Sinatra was but they understood he was famous and that it was a secret.

When the children were in bed I told Julia about going undercover and pretending to be man and wife with Ian. She asked me if I was afraid. I said, "I'm frightened we will get rumbled. And what will happen to us if we do. Sinatra is supposed to have mafia connections. He could cause us serious harm if he wanted."

She said, "I meant aren't you nervous about sharing a room with a man you've never met before?"

We dug out a Frank Sinatra tape and sang along and giggled through 'Strangers in the Night' and a bottle of red wine.

The next day, waiting for me in the office was a FedEx envelope from Ian with the schedule of events for the Magic Carpet Weekend with the Sinatras.

Friday, May 20, 1988

6:00 p.m. Arrive Las Vegas – Guests will be met and taken to Bally's Casino Resort by limousine. Luggage will be delivered to your preassigned suite.

8:00 p.m. Cocktails – Metro 1 (26th Floor)

8:30 p.m. Dinner – Metro 2 (26th Floor)

10.30 p.m. Guests will be escorted to the Ziegfeld Room to attend Donn Arden's $10m dollar extravaganza "Jubilee!"

11:00 p.m. Showtime.

Dress: Moderately dressy (not cocktail dress).

Ties not required but suggested.

Saturday, May 21, 1988

No planned activities for the morning. Golf and tennis is available but advance notice is required.

12:00 p.m. For the Ladies, small informal luncheon and Norman Marcus fashion show. Meet Paul-Louis Orrier in person and see his Fall/Winter '88 collection – to be held in the Gables 6 and 7 ballroom on the third floor of the Tracy Tower (take escalator).

Dress: Casual, sporting attire or slacks.

2:30 p.m. Luncheon finished – no planned activities for the afternoon.

7:00 p.m. Cocktails and Hors d'Oeuvres. Metro 1 (26th Floor)

8:00 p.m. Guests will be escorted to the Celebrity Room – Dean Martin Show.

8:30 p.m. Showtime

10:00 p.m. Guests will be escorted to Metro 2 (26th Floor)

10:30 p.m. Dinner – Metro 2.

Sunday, May 22, 1988

2:00 p.m. – 3.30 p.m. Champagne Brunch, Sinatra's restaurant on second floor of Tracy Tower (take escalator)

3:30 p.m. Guests to be escorted to limousines for departure from Las Vegas airport.

4:00 p.m. Depart Las Vegas.

Before all of that we were invited to join the Sinatra's at their home in Palm Springs and travel with them on their private jet to Las

Vegas. It was mind blowing. It was getting more and more surreal. Three whole days of being undercover 24/7.

What on earth was I going to wear to all these events? And I was going to have to pretend I was rich right from the start. I couldn't turn up to the Sinatra's house in my usual travelling scruffs.

I wrote a list of what I would need. It included a dress for the meet and greet at the Sinatra's home, a dress for the Friday evening. What on earth did moderately dressy mean? And then Saturday: casual, sporting attire or slacks.

I began to feel unsure. If we didn't look the part we would immediately arouse suspicion. I rang Ian. He told me he was having a couple of suits made especially so he would look fittingly dapper. I waylaid Peter Miller and said I had received the programme, there were several events and I would need the right clothes. He wasn't that bothered. "Just sort it Sandra."

"Just sort it," was the approval I needed to go shopping.

That lunchtime I darted to a massive department store in Oxford Street. In one huge space they had hundreds of dresses by different designers. I raced up the escalator and whizzed round the gowns like I was in that TV programme 'Supermarket Sweep.' At ninety miles an hour I dashed in and out of changing rooms and splashed out several hundred pounds on a couple of Frank Usher evening dresses and some Jacques Vert dresses.

I ran to the shoe department and spent another few hundred pounds on shoes and bags. Then I hot footed it to the lingerie department and gave my credit card another battering, kitting myself out with exquisite bras, French knickers, suspender belts and stockings. Well, I was going to be sharing a room with a man I hadn't yet met.

The morning of my flight, I went to get my hair done and I panic bought a Kanga dress from a little exclusive boutique at the end of Sevenoaks High Street. Lady "Kanga" Tryon was an Australian designer who was a close friend of Prince Charles. Princess Diana was a fan and wore one of her dresses to the Live Aid concert at Wembley stadium in 1985.

At Heathrow, before I boarded the flight, I rang the office. My previous briefings had been exactly that – brief. No-one knew if we would get in or not. If we did, and we managed to stay undercover, we would have a great story to tell. If we didn't – well, who knew what would happen to us. Sinatra was a very powerful man. It didn't bear thinking about. Bill Hagerty, the deputy editor and a massive Sinatra fan, just said, "Good luck Sandra."

The British Airways flight was half empty so I had a row to myself. I stretched out and listened to Frank Sinatra tapes on my Walkman and made my way through some of the Kitty Kelly bestseller, His Way The Unauthorized Biography of Frank Sinatra, which had been published 18 months previously. It was a warts and all account of the great man which had received good reviews, although not from the Sinatra clan. I read about his early life in a poor area outside New York and his relationship with his powerful mother and his attempts to make it as a singer. I felt relaxed and prepared by the time we landed in Los Angeles 12 hours later.

Ian was going to meet me and, as he didn't know what I looked like, I told him I would be wearing my usual travelling outfit: pink tracksuit bottoms and a white T shirt with 'Hello Sailor' spelled out in pink sequins. Ian had asked, "Hello Sailor?"

I laughed. "It's comfortable!"

As I reached the immigration desk I handed over my passport and the immigration form they hand out on the plane. The immigration officer noticed I had left blank the address of where I would be staying.

"You need to fill in the address where you're staying Ma'am," he instructed.

I couldn't. I explained I would be staying with a colleague and he was meeting me but he hadn't told me his address.

The burly immigration officer wasn't impressed. "You must know where you're going to be staying."

"I'm sorry I don't. I know I am staying somewhere in LA but apart from that I don't know any more." For some reason the immigration guy thought this was suspicious and waved over an even bigger colleague who marched me off to a tiny office. Two other unfriendly immigration officers demanded to know why I didn't know where I would be staying. I went through everything again but no matter how many times they asked me for my address in LA, I didn't have a clue.

"Look," I said, "Ian is out there waiting for me. If you page him, he will come forward and you can ask his address."

"That's not gonna happen Ma'am."

They asked me what I was doing in LA. I said, sort of truthfully, that I was going to do some showbiz interviews. I could hardly say I was going undercover to sneak into Frank Sinatra's house.

I was trying to work out what the time was in London. If the office was open I could ring them and get Ian's address out of the accounts department. If the office was closed, I had been given Bill Hagerty's home number in case of an emergency, I could ring him and get him to verify what I was saying. I really didn't want to do that but things were looking desperate. I asked if I could make a phone call.

"That's not gonna happen Ma'am."

"Well, what is going to happen?" I asked, trying to keep calm.

"Right now Ma'am, we're looking at getting you on the next flight back to London."

"What?"

I was shocked. I couldn't believe it. Just because I didn't know the address of where I was staying I was being thrown out of the US. The office had spent a fortune and it looked as though all I would be doing was a round trip to Heathrow. I would surely be fired. I felt ill.

"Surely I can make a phone call?"

"No Ma'am." At least they were polite!

I was desperate. I don't know why but I asked, "Can I see someone from British Airways please?"

Half an hour later the door opened and a boisterous woman in the familiar red, white and blue BA uniform breezed in. "They want you on the next flight out. What's all this about?"

I explained I was getting deported because I didn't know the address where I would be living, that I was being met by the man I was going to stay with.

She raised her eyebrows. "Have you stayed with him before?"

"No. We haven't met yet. This is the first time."

"You've come to LA to stay with a man you've never met before?"

She was looking at me as though she was my mother. I tried to explain without saying much. "He's a colleague. We're going to be working together and he invited me to stay with him."

Shaking her head, she picked up my immigration card. I watched wide-eyed as she filled in the missing information.

Handing it back to me, she said, "There. That's my address. They don't need to know that. Tell them you have remembered where you will be staying."

I was dumbfounded. "Do you really think this is going to work? I have been in here for over two hours telling them I don't know the address. Now I'm supposed to have suddenly remembered it."

"You haven't got a choice. It is your only chance."

She swept out and the two immigration officers sauntered in. "So, you have remembered where you are staying?"

"Yes," I lied.

They picked up the immigration card, read the address and asked, "Where will you be staying?"

I had one chance at this. I had quickly looked at the address as the BA woman had written it, now I had to remember it. I recited an address of a condominium in LA as my two interrogators studied the card.

"Mmmm." I could tell they weren't convinced but, incredibly, they declared, "OK ma'am you're free to go. Sorry to have delayed you. Come with us."

They led me back into immigration and took me straight to the front of a queue at one of the desks, where their colleague stamped my passport as if nothing had happened. "Welcome to America ma'am. Have a good day."

When I eventually made it through, Ian was still there waiting patiently. We shook hands, a bit formal for someone I was going to stay with, but we are British!

"What happened?" he asked.

He knew I had arrived because from where he was standing he could see the immigration hall and spotted my sparkly 'Hello Sailor" T shirt. Thank goodness for pink sequins! He realised there was a problem when I was marched off but he had no idea what it was. He was as surprised as I was when I told him the immigration officials had accepted I had suddenly remembered the address and let me through. They looked at my immigration card as though they were seeing it for the first time. Unbelievable!

Ian understood my trauma of almost being deported and our massively expensive assignment failing before it had even begun. We thought our biggest hurdle was going to be getting accepted by the Sinatras, not getting in to the US. But I'd made it and I was keen to get away from the airport as quickly as possible before anyone changed their mind. Ian had a brand new bright red Mazda 5 sports car. Blimey! Here was I worried about my Selfridges splurge and Ian had bought a car! We piled my bags into the back and sped away.

I was relieved that Ian was easy to talk to. He was a well-respected former Fleet Street staffer, a friendly faced Scot, who the Americans thought sounded like Sean Connery. We both admitted we were nervous at what the Sunday Mirror was expecting us to pull off. But we were excitedly looking forward to it.

Ian thought the best way for me to deal with jet lag was to try to stay awake, so he drove us out of LA and along the coast road to Santa Monica where we stopped at a fabulous seafood restaurant overlooking the ocean. I had assumed Ian lived in LA but he told me he lived in the hills above Santa Monica. Eventually, full of shrimps and lobster, we left the ocean behind and made our way along the bumpy roads winding their way through the hills, up and up through barren landscapes until we reached 2882 Hume Road, standing alone in the scrub. All I could see from the road was a tall grey weather worn fence and electric wooden gates. As we drove through the gates we were met by a beautiful higgledy-piggledy wooden house clinging to the hillside and surrounded by verandas that had breathtaking views down the canyon to the sea.

"Do you like it?" Ian asked.

"It's stunning," I replied.

"It belongs to a friend of mine," Ian explained, "Jeff Bridges."

"Jeff Bridges?" Did Ian really mean the film star Jeff Bridges? Gorgeous, good looking star of films like Starman, Tron and Jagged Edge. He did.

As we lifted my cases out of the Mazda Ian told me he had been friends with Jeff Bridges since they hit it off when he interviewed him several years previously. This house had been the Bridges family home until they had outgrown it and had recently moved to a mansion closer to Hollywood. Jeff was hanging on to it for his young children but in the meantime he let Ian stay there.

Downstairs the house was open plan, apart from a bedroom with an en suite bathroom which is where I would be staying. From the living room, there was a ladder up to a mezzanine floor where Ian's bedroom and bathroom were. There was a staircase outside the house which also led to this mezzanine floor and a shower like I had never seen before. It was outside, on the roof, made completely of glass, like a small conservatory. You could shower taking in the incredible views but, as there were no neighbours, no-one could see you. Whichever bougainvillea-framed window you looked through there was a fantastic view. Although I was London born and bred and a town girl, I fell in love with this house in the middle of nowhere and the open starkness of the surrounding area. It was so peaceful.

I couldn't sleep. I don't know if it was just jet lag, the futon bed Ian had bought especially for me, or the excitement of being in Jeff Bridges' house and about to meet Frank Sinatra. I tried to read my Kitty Kelly book but I couldn't concentrate. I tossed and turned.

Ian and I had six days to get our story straight. We decided to keep it simple and as near to the truth as possible. I was a writer in England. I couldn't move to live permanently with Ian because I had two young children from a previous marriage. He came to the UK as often as he could. We hadn't been married for very long and, so far, we were coping with our long distance relationship. We memorised each other's birthdays, our wedding date (which we made my parents' wedding date of April 3), how we met, anything we could think of that might come up in small talk over pre-dinner drinks or around the table. We agreed that if one of us got into a sticky situation we would find each other and by holding hands we would alert the other one that we needed help. We settled into a routine of learning our "lines," supermarket shopping, cooking, going to the cinema, watching TV with a glass of wine. We had become the married couple we were pretending to be.

We bombed around LA in the Mazda in the warm May sunshine with Frank Sinatra tapes playing at full pelt to get us into the spirit of the upcoming weekend. I settled on 'The Summer Wind' as my favourite. It's a beautiful song and it seemed apt: here I was a long way from home, in distance and lifestyle, enjoying the summer wind playing havoc with my hair as we drove along the ocean road. It was almost like being on holiday. But I wasn't.

Ian introduced me to some charming friends of his who lived nearby, Dan and Darling McVicar. Dan was a struggling actor who had recently landed a part in a daytime soap. They invited us round for a meal while we watched one of his first appearances. We laughed as Dan's first scene had him hiding in a wardrobe because his lover's husband had returned home unexpectedly. Dan hoped the character, Clarke Garrison, would get called back for other episodes. The soap was the world famous The Bold and the Beautiful.

11

The more time I spent there, the more I adored Jeff's wooden house, the area, California, the climate, the lovely people I met. But I missed my children. I had to work to support us but my work meant I was often away from home. While I was working I had to be focused and strong. When I wasn't working, when I was alone in my room, I would get out my photos of the children, hug and kiss them and very often cry. If my children had been with me I don't think I would have ever gone home.

During the few days we had before leaving for our assignment, Jeff Bridges invited us round to his new mansion near Beverly Hills.

We rolled up to the electric gates in the Mazda and Ian spoke into the intercom. By the time we had parked on the drive, Jeff Bridges, superstar, had opened the massive wooden front door of the Spanish style villa and was calling to us, "Come on, come in."

He was taller than I imagined and his shaggy hair framed laughing eyes. He was dressed casually in slacks and an open necked shirt and plodded around in bare feet.

While his Scottish nanny brought us some tea, he asked, "Seen Frank yet?" Ian explained that we hadn't done it yet, our assignment was in a couple of days. Jeff wanted to hear all about it and found the whole situation amusing. He was charming, welcoming, and even sexier in real life, with a mischievous twinkle in his eye.

Jeff warned us, "You know Frank hates the press."

We said, "We're not press, we're wealthy British fans."

Jeff laughed but he didn't seem convinced. He asked, "Are you afraid?"

"Afraid of what?"

"Frank?"

"Frank? Why? What could he do to us?"

"Frank can do whatever he wants."

The more I read of the Kitty Kelly book, the more nervous I became. She wrote about Frank Sinatra's womanising, his mafia connections, people who upset him getting concrete boots. She presented him as a thoroughly unpleasant, scary person. I decided not to read anymore.

I still couldn't sleep. Now I didn't know if it was due to the excitement of having met Jeff Bridges, fear of concrete boots, or jet lag, but I was getting worried. I knew I needed some sleep to be on top form during a very challenging assignment which was getting frighteningly close.

The night before we left we went to a vodka and caviar bar. That's all they served. The vodka came in shot glasses sitting in a saucer of ice. The caviar was also served in tiny saucers. Much, much later we took a taxi home and, unbelievably, considering what we were about to do, but thanks to the vodka, I slept like a log.

In the morning I painted my nails and laid on my bed in my beautiful new underwear while the varnish dried, focusing on the job we had to do. When we emerged a while later we were Mr and Mrs Black, wealthy Brits going to the Sinatras for the weekend. Ian wore a beautifully tailored suit and a crisp new shirt. I had decided to wear a loose fitting royal blue Jacques Vert jersey dress which I thought would be comfortable for travelling.

Watched by Ian, I placed my wedding ring and my mother's sapphire and diamond engagement ring on my left hand. The pretence was complete.

I called the office to tell them we would be leaving shortly. Bill Hagerty, said simply, "Good luck."

Then he added, "Sandra, if ever it looks dodgy get out of there fast." So he'd read the Kitty Kelly book too.

Dan McVicar, Jeff Bridges and other friends of Ian called to wish us luck. They were all as excited as we were and wanted to hear from us as soon as we got back. It was amazing that someone as famous as Jeff Bridges who rubbed shoulders with the big names of Hollywood wanted to hear what Frank was really like. Not many people had got to know the real Frank Sinatra – or had even met him.

When the limo pulled up at the gates to take us to the airport, the chauffeur held the door open for me. I slid into the luxurious leather seats. We were dressed for it. It suited us.

We were on our way.

TWO

Frank and Barbara Sinatra sent a limo to collect us at Palm Springs airport and take us the 20 minute drive to their home on Frank Sinatra Drive in Rancho Mirage, a celebrity filled development of luxury homes where the lush greens of the golf courses sat incongruously in the scorched Californian desert.

The limo slowed alongside a huge neatly trimmed privet hedge; a stone wall framed the wide electric gates, dominated by security cameras on tall posts – the kind you see lining the perimeter in prison movies. Ian and I knew this was crunch time. We would either get in or be sent away. Or worse. The gates slowly – agonisingly slowly - pulled back, the limo edged forward and two armed security guards appeared from the guard house tucked inside the gate on the right. The driver operated the limo windows. Ian and I both reached out for each other's hand. We held tightly on to each other as the guards put their heads through the window. "Mr. and Mrs. Black. Welcome to the Sinatra residence." We breathed a secret, silent sigh of relief.

The Sinatra house, known as The Compound, was a series of fairly ordinary looking white single story buildings set in grounds with carefully tended flower beds, a tennis court and a pool.

We were escorted to the room the Sinatras call their theatre by the chauffeur. It is the room where the Sinatras entertain their friends. Or, in this case, those of us who had shelled out a vast amount of money to be in the same room as Ol' Blue Eyes. As we entered, the man himself jumped up and greeted us like old friends.

"Welcome Sandra and Ian," he said extending his hand.

Barbara urged, "Come in. Welcome." It was extraordinary, like they had known us for years.

Frank was shorter than I had imagined but he held himself tall and straight.

Moving towards the bar at the side of the room, Frank asked me, "What would you like to drink?" I really wanted a stiff gin but I didn't think that would be a good idea so I asked for an orange juice. With that, Frank theatrically waved his arm and, pointing to the door, ordered, "Out!" Everyone laughed, obviously he wasn't expecting anyone to not be drinking this weekend.

He looked happy and relaxed in a cream open necked shirt and dark trousers, much younger than his 72 years. The paleness of his shirt emphasised his legendry blue eyes. They really were blue, a piercing ice cool blue.

There were several guests already sipping drinks and making small talk, as orchestrated Beatles classics played softly in the background. The other guests for the weekend were Sinatra's close friends who I thought had been leant on to support Barbara's charity. We were completely taken aback to find some English people there. The Magic Carpet Weekend had made just one paragraph in the Daily Mail newspaper's diary column but it had been spotted by a wealthy businessman from north London who had bought the weekend as a birthday surprise for his wife. Their pregnant daughter had come along too. We would have to give them a wide berth. They, of any of the guests, would be harder to fool. They could ask us the sort of prying questions about England and London, about our relationship, our jobs, that could expose us. Ian and I exchanged a brief knowing glance.

Frank explained that the mother and daughter's luggage had gone astray but they needn't worry, "I've got people on to it." I bet he did. I wouldn't like to be the airline rep getting a call from Frank Sinatra.

The only person I recognised was British entertainer, Dudley Moore of Pete n' Dud fame. He was accompanied by his third wife Brogan Lane who towered over diminutive Dud. They had recently wed in Las Vegas. As he lived in LA, Ian recognised other guests including Mike Connors, star of Mannix, Hollywood producer Leo Jaffe and Sinatra's old friend, the singing cowboy Gene Autry. Jilly Rizzo, Frank's oldest friend, stood quietly weighing us all up. I tried to not look guilty.

Barbara told us James Bond star Roger Moore and his wife Luisa were supposed to have been there but her father had just died.

Frank stayed by my side. I admired a large black and white abstract painting dominating the room. It was striking. It was the first thing you noticed, after Frank.

"I did that. I only just finished it."

I said, "I didn't realise you were an artist?"

"Well, I'm not sure I would call myself an artist. I like to paint. I can go to my studio and lose myself in painting. Barbara encourages me. I think she likes it when I disappear to paint. It gets me out of her hair for a while."

Barbara nodded her agreement. Barbara was a former Las Vegas showgirl who met Sinatra while she was still married to Zeppo, one of the legendary Marx Brothers comedians. They were neighbours, just across the golf course.

She was a glamourous 56-year-old, who looked cool and elegant in a cream trouser suit. She matched the cream and white décor of the room: white walls, white and cream tub armchairs and sofas. Everything was white, including the sunken bar. Much of the walls were covered by dozens of mostly black and white photographs of Sinatra with his famous friends, including his Rat Pack cronies, Dean Martin and Sammy Davies Jnr., and mementoes of his more than 50 albums and 60 movies.

I was being shown around the place by one of the most – if not THE most – famous men in the world. It oozed memories. A who's who of Hollywood had been in this same room over the years. It was Frank's inner sanctum where he took his friends and lovers. Marilyn Monroe, Ava Gardner and even President John F. Kennedy had all been in this room, sipping their drinks just like me.

At one end of the long room was a cinema screen shielded by curtains where Frank liked to show his friends movies that hadn't yet been released. At the other end was a drop down TV screen where he watched his favourite TV shows 'Jeopardy!' and 'Wheel of Fortune.'

The room was more comfortable than opulent. Not Hollywood at all. Totally in keeping with Frank coming home, kicking off his shoes and relaxing.

The Magic Carpet Weekend with the Sinatras was a more public display of Frank's generosity. He told me he preferred to support causes privately, "But this is going to be fun. Giving is my pleasure."

Barbara thanked me for coming all the way from England to support her charity. She told us the Magic Carpet Weekend was raising money for a centre for sexually abused children she had set up at the nearby Eisenhower Hospital. She said, "Do you realise that over 90 per cent of all the people in jail in this and in many other countries were sexually or mentally abused children?

"Their self worth is so low. If we can work on this we can really change society."

Although Frank Sinatra had donated $250,000 of his own money to the centre plus proceeds from his concerts, Barbara told us he is banned from actually going there.

Barbara explained that molesting fathers often attend the centre for treatment. "My husband's from a totally different school. He wants to break their legs."

I smiled, not knowing whether to believe her or not.

"Really," she said, "he wants to round up all these men and break their legs."

Frank smiled, a twinkle in his famous eyes, and, looking like butter wouldn't melt in his mouth, he said, "You can talk to these guys all you want but let me teach them a lesson and they will NEVER do it again.

"If you put them in a hospital for a year, when they come out they won't be molesting kids any more."

He was serious. Ian and I grabbed each other's hand. What would Frank do to us if he found out who we really were?

Barbara shook her head. Frank insisted, "I'm telling you I'm right."

Then he suddenly grabbed my hand and said, "Sandra, come and see my trains." Ian followed. Dudley and Brogan were standing by the door. "Come on," Frank said to them, "Come with us."

I was surprised that Dudley seemed shy. He seemed in awe of Frank and tongue-tied. Frank hastily introduced us and led us out of the theatre. I walked beside Frank along a narrow flower-lined concrete path. Dudley whispered to Ian, "Where are we going?"

"Trains," Ian replied. Dudley giggled.

We walked through a hedge past a caboose, a conductor's cabin from the end of a freight train, which was given to him by his loyal staff, who always called him Mr.S. A metal plaque read: "Mr. Sinatra, strength, kindness and integrity." It's where the barber came to trim his hair and the masseuse gave him relaxing massages.

Before us, in a quiet corner of the garden, stood a little, brown wooden shack. Frank nodded to a wooden rocking chair on the veranda. "I like to sit there and think.

"The house is a replica of the house I grew up in in Hoboken."

The slums of Hoboken are a long way from Palm Springs but Frank still hankered after his home town. "In Hoboken if you had a veranda you'd made it! I built this one to remind me. When I sit here it is though I am miles away from anywhere. It's so peaceful."

He pushed open the door to his haven and smiled. "Come in, this is my fairyland."

The sight was staggering: Frank Sinatra King of Las Vegas, collects model trains. The shack was packed from floor to ceiling with shelves containing hundreds of them. A multi-million dollar collection of neatly arranged tiny trains.

In the centre of the shack was a large model railway layout which Frank had built himself. "I keep changing it and adding to it," he beamed, "It is a replica of the famous Lionel showroom in New York."

He led us around the layout. Dudley was still giggling. At one end was a little village of coloured town houses covered in snow but on the other side of the papier mache hills it was summertime. There were tracks on two levels which wound round houses, factories, mountains and bridges. Eight trains could go round the tracks at once. "Look," Frank pointed to a miniature Hoboken. A tiny billboard advertised one of his sell out concerts. On the far side were the controls and a red and black engine driver's hat he wore when he played with his train set and an engine driver's whistle. He explained he wasn't always alone. "When I feel like playing with my trains I get a few of the neighbourhood kids in. They come down here from the poorer part of town and we have a wow of a time. Can you imagine their faces when they see this? Their eyes are like pool balls. They think it is just great.

"We all take turns at being engine driver and sometimes I fix it so the trains crash just so I can see their reaction. They think I am going to blow up, but I just laugh."

As we did a circuit of the train set, Frank told us he has been collecting model trains since he was a boy and had some from all over the world. He showed us an engine that had been a gift from the Vatican and a cut glass model of the train that inspired the Glenn Miller song 'Chattanooga Choo Choo." Among his favourites was one that Barbara had given him for Christmas. Pointing to a large, solid brass antique train, that Barbara bought in England, he said, "She just saw it in a shop window and bought it back for me. She also had this one made for me. Its crystal, look at the way they have cut the wheels. Barbara is fantastic to think of presents like this. I adore her."

Another of his favourites must also have been the most valuable. It was a solid gold model of an early American engine which had his initials, "FAS," picked out in diamonds and rubies. He pushed his nose sideways, to give himself a broken nose look, imitating "heavies."

"It's from the boys downtown."

The train he liked to play with the most was a high speed Japanese train, a model of one he had travelled on many times.

Replicas of every plane he had ever owned hung from the wooden ceiling. On the wall was a plaque which read: "He Who Has the Most Toys Wins."

We had already done a circuit of the model village when Frank started the tour again, pointing out the same things he had shown us first time. Dudley could hardly contain his giggles and Brogan nudged him in the ribs. They were like a couple of naughty school kids.

Eventually Frank said, "Well, time to get this show on the road," and we followed him back to the main house.

As we all sauntered back into the theatre we could sense the envy of the other guests. We had spent most of the meet and greet time alone with Frank. Mike Connors sidled up to me and whispered, "Do you realise how special that was? Frank must like you. Very few of his friends have been allowed to see his trains."

Barbara was fussing around us, urging us all to make a move, it was time to go. Mike Connors said, "That's how Sinatra rules his life. On time. If Frank says its wheels up at 5.15, then we leave at 5.15. Not a minute sooner, not a minute later.

"If he says he wants his pizza on the table at 9.10, he walks in at 9.09."

We were escorted down the path to the convoy of limos waiting to take us to the airport. With military precision the cavalcade of limos left The Compound - on time.

In fact, the Boeing 737 that had been chartered for this Magic Carpet ride left a few minutes late but there were no Sinatra tantrums. Sitting across the aisle from Ian and I, Frank buried his head into a newspaper until take-off.

As the plane left the tarmac, he looked out of the window to his left and became sad. It was the only time throughout the weekend that I saw him without a smile or a twinkle in his eyes. He told me later, "I was saying a silent prayer. Whenever we take off from Palm Springs, whether we turn left or right, I look at those hills and think of my dear old Mom."

He told me his mother, Dolly, was killed in a plane crash on those same mountains on January 6, 1977. Sinatra declared, "That's my religion these days – if god wants you, he takes you, that's all there is to it."

As we landed in Las Vegas, Frank stood up and, laughing, pulled on a black blouson jacket, turning his back to us so we could all see the inscription written in silver silk on the back: "I Wanna Go Home."

But there was no turning back. At Las Vegas airport another convoy of limos was waiting to take us the 15 minute drive to the Bally Hotel and Casino Resort, one of the best known and glamourous in the world.

Incredibly, traffic was halted to let our Presidential-like cavalcade pass. Sitting behind the blacked out windows of a gleaming black limo, driving by stopped cars, I thought this must be how it is for The Queen or the President.

As we pulled up outside the grand hotel entrance, we were greeted by crowds held back by armed guards and security men with walkie-talkies. A smiling valet came to meet us. "Mr and Mrs Black, welcome to Bally's, please let me show you to your room."

Suite 7310 was the biggest hotel room I had ever seen. It felt as big as a football pitch and had massive windows overlooking the busyness of Vegas. The lounge was elegant, with thick carpet, several plush, grey sofas, a massive TV and a well stocked bar in the corner. On the highly polished coffee table was an arrangement of fresh flowers with a card reading: "To Sandra and Ian, from Barbara and Frank Sinatra." There was a huge bowl of fruit and a box containing four beautiful crystal cut glass wine glasses, a gift from the Sinatras.

The room, as big as many apartments, was open plan: the bedroom was up a carpeted step and contained a bed much larger than a King size.

We stood there staring at it. Ian declared, "I'm not sleeping on the sofa."

There would be no need for that. We could easily sleep separately in this bed which would be safer for maintaining our story. To the right of the bed, up another step, was the marble tiled bathroom, complete with sunken bath surrounded by wardrobes, huge mirrors and the shower and toilet cubicle.

Ian and I stood in the middle of the room, taking it all in, slightly dazed by the day's events. We hugged each other and laughed. We were relieved to have got this far. We talked about the scary moments: the armed guards peering in at us, the English women, and Frank wanting to break the legs of sex offenders!

We knew Frank taking us on a tour of his trains would make a good story. One step at a time, but it had been a good start.

I changed from my blue dress into trousers and plain sweat shirt and, leaving Ian unpacking, I made my way down to the garish red and gold hotel lobby. The hotel was a maze of escalators. I just kept on going down. I didn't know where I was going and I was worried in case I couldn't find my way back. Eventually I ended up in a room full of slot machines. No-one paid any attention to me; everyone had their heads down playing the one armed bandits. Waitresses were serving drinks and security men were wandering around, but I looked just like another tourist. Eventually on the far wall, I saw what I was looking for: a public telephone.

Checking that no-one could see or hear me, I dialled Bill Hagerty's number. "It's Sandra."

"Yes?"

"We're in."

There was a lengthy pause.

"Sandra. I envy you."

"Yes."

"Sandra."

"Yes?"

"Be careful."

BARBARA SINATRA CHILDREN'S CENTER
AT
EISENHOWER

May 6, 1988

Mr. and Mrs. Ian Black
2882 Hume Road
Malibu, California 90265

Dear Mr. and Mrs. Black:

Thank you very much for your generous donation of $25,000 to the Children's Center Endowment Fund for our May 20, 1988 Las Vegas weekend.

Because of the generosity of Bally's-Las Vegas hotel in hosting our "Magic Carpet Weekend", and other Underwriters, the full amount of each couple's contribution will go to the Fund, thus insuring the continued care and treatment of sexually and physically abused children, regardless of their ability to pay.

The enclosed information about the Center will give you a better understanding about our program.

Again, on behalf of the children who will benefit from your meaningful gift, and from all of us at the Center, our heartfelt thanks for your support.

Sincerely,

Barbara Sinatra

PRESIDENT

lw
encl. Receipt No. 1934

EISENHOWER MEDICAL CENTER
39000 BOB HOPE DRIVE · RANCHO MIRAGE, CALIFORNIA 92270 · 619 / 340-2336

Letter from Barbara Sinatra thanking us for our "donation" to her children's charity.

Frank and Barbara Sinatra on the cover of the special invitation.

Barbara and Frank Sinatra
Invite You to Join Them
for
A "Magic Carpet Weekend"
in Las Vegas
Friday, May 20
Saturday, May 21
and
Sunday, May 22
1988

hosted by

Bally's – Las Vegas

This magical weekend with the Sinatras will be three exciting days of parties, shows and surprises that you'll never forget!

You'll fly to Las Vegas on Friday on a luxurious, private plane. The party begins in the air and continues as waiting limousines whisk you to the fabulous Bally's–Las Vegas hotel for your V.I.P. check-in to your lavish suite of rooms.

Cocktails, dinner and a show, the million-dollar "Jubilee" extravaganza will follow that evening. Saturday it's another party, dinner and the "Dean Martin Show!"

In between, there'll be plenty of time to relax and enjoy shopping, sunning, golf or tennis. On Sunday, there'll be a wonderful Champagne Brunch before your "magic carpet" flight home. No detail has been overlooked in planning this memorable three-day holiday. Make your reservation soon!

Limited to 25 Couples
$25,000 per couple

R.V.P. Card Enclosed

Our special invitation.

27

Bally's Casino Resort is proud to host

A Magic Carpet Weekend
with the Sinatras

For the Benefit of the
Barbara Sinatra Children's Center at Eisenhower

BALLY'S
CASINO RESORT · LAS VEGAS

Cover of the schedule of events at Bally's Casino Resort.

SCHEDULE OF EVENTS

Friday, May 20, 1988

6:00 p.m. Arrive Las Vegas — Guests will be met and taken to Bally's Casino Resort by limousine. Luggage will be delivered directly to your preassigned suite.

8:00 p.m. Cocktails — Metro 1 (26th Floor)

8:30 p.m. Dinner — Metro 2 (26th Floor)

10:30 p.m. Guests will be escorted to the Ziegfeld Room to attend Donn Arden's $10 million dollar extravaganza "Jubilee!"

11:00 p.m. Showtime
Dress: Moderately dressy (not cocktail dress).
Ties not required but suggested.

Saturday, May 21, 1988

No planned activities for the morning. Golf and Tennis is available but advance notice is required.

Saturday, May 21, 1988 (Continued)

12:00 p.m. For the Ladies, small informal luncheon and Neiman Marcus fashion show. Meet Paul-Louis Orrier in person and see his Fall/Winter '88 collection — to be held in Gables 6 and 7 Ballroom on the third floor of the Tracy Tower (take escalator).
Dress: Casual, sporting attire or slacks.

2:30 p.m. Luncheon finished — no planned activities for the afternoon

7:00 p.m. Cocktails and Hors d'Oeuvres, Metro 1 (26th Floor).

8:00 p.m. Guests will be escorted to the Celebrity Room—Dean Martin Show

8:30 p.m. Showtime

10:00 p.m. Guests will be escorted to Metro 2 (26th Floor)

10:30 p.m. Dinner — Metro 2

Sunday, May 22, 1988

2:00 p.m.- 3:30 p.m. Champagne Brunch, Sinatra's Restaurant on second floor of Tracy Tower (take escalator).

3:30 p.m. Guests to be escorted to limousines for departure from Las Vegas airport.

4:00 p.m. Depart Las Vegas

NOTE: Luggage should be ready for pickup by 1:30 p.m. as it will be delivered to the airport ahead of our arrival.

IMPORTANT: If you need assistance of any kind or have any questions, call La Donna Webb 794-2415 (our contacts here or dial List 1 digits from inside direct) or have the hotel operator help.

Our schedule of events at Bally's Casino and Resort.

29

Me and Ian. I'm wearing the Kanga dress Frank liked.

*Me with Mike Connors, his wife Marylou and Mary
Kickerillo.*

Me with Frank Sinatra.

Me holding hands with Ol'Blue Eyes.

May 24, 1988

Dear Sandra and Ian,

It was a wonderful, warm, exciting weekend in Las Vegas and we hope you enjoyed it as much as we enjoyed having you with us!

Hopefully, we will have many beautiful pictures of our moments together and when they are ready we will send them to you.

Again, our heartfelt thanks for your support of the Center. Your generosity will help us keep our promise that "no child will be turned away because of financial hardship."

Have a wonderful summer!

Love,

Barbara

Mr. and Mrs. Ian Black
2882 Hume Road
Malibu, California 90265

Thank you letter from Barbara Sinatra.

THREE

For our first evening I decided to wear the Kanga dress I had bought last minute in Sevenoaks. I wanted to be comfortable and it was easy to wear. The schedule said "moderately dressy, not cocktail dress" and it fitted the bill perfectly. It had a loose top, which could be worn off the shoulder if you felt daring, and was gathered on the hips, almost 1920's style. The fabric was a deep turquoise with pink flowers. I added the cameo ring my parents had given me for my 21st (actually, the replacement: I had accidentally put the original one down a waste disposal unit), a multi coloured gold bracelet my colleagues had given me when I left the Daily Star, and an antique ivory necklace. I knew I wouldn't be able to compete with the other ladies who, no doubt, would be decked out in very expensive bling, but I thought my jewellery was tasteful, a bit quirky and understated – very British. Ian wore an expensive blue suit and a shirt and tie. We looked each other up and down and decided we looked the part.

"Ready?" Ian asked.

"Ready." I answered.

We had to meet in Metro 1 on the 26th Floor of Bally's for cocktails at 8pm followed by dinner in Metro 2 at 8.30pm. When Frank arrived and saw I was drinking a glass of champagne he pointed at my glass and grinned. "Ah, that's better."

Dudley Moore played the piano as we mingled with the other guests, who now included Barbara's 6ft 4in tall, good looking son Bobby Marx. The small talk wasn't too delving. Mike Connor's wife, Marylou, asked where we had met, how we managed with a long distance relationship, questions we had expected and rehearsed. We stuck to our prepared story. Mike said to me, "You've made a hit with Frank. He thinks you are intriguing." We laughed at 'intriguing.'

I don't know how I had managed to be a hit with Frank, other than I did my best to look interested and ask lots of questions as he was showing us around his trains.

Everything was going well until Barbara came rushing up to us followed closely by a security guard. "There's a problem," she declared.

A problem? It must be us. Ian and I held hands. I thought concrete boots. I hoped I wasn't giving anything away. At school I was always one of those kids who went red, guilty or not, whenever someone had misbehaved.

"I am insulted," an irate Barbara went on. Ian and I did not speak. The security guard behind her shook his head.

"Frank is very annoyed," Barbara told us. We looked across at Frank who was talking to another security guard. "Can you believe this?" she asked, "those English women have sneaked into where we are having dinner and swapped the place cards around. They saw that they weren't on Frank's table and changed the cards so that they were. I caught them. I caught them red handed."

Phew! Ian and I visibly relaxed. "Sorry," we mumbled, "we are embarrassed that they are English. Hope you don't think we are all like that?"

Barbara smiled. "No, no, of course not. I am shocked that they would do such a thing. I went to check on everything and caught them doing it. It is insulting." Ian and I nodded.

Barbara continued, "Well, Frank won't have those women near him now. He is refusing to have them on his table the whole weekend." Ian and I smiled in agreement.

The English mother and daughter were the talk of the room. Their crass behaviour had taken the heat off us. Unbelievably, the two women carried on brazenly sipping their drinks while the drama unfolded.

As we were ushered into the private dining room, Barbara escorted me to my seat. "You're sitting here, Sandra, next to Frank," she said loud enough for the two English women to hear. I couldn't believe my luck. There were four tables in the room. Ian and I could have been on any one of them. Thanks to those two English women, not only were Ian and I on Frank's table, I was sitting right beside him. Right next to Ol' Blue Eyes, the legend. What a result! But part of me realised it also put pressure on me to maintain our story.

While a harpist played popular tunes, we ate fabulous food washed down with fine wines. It was obvious that Frank was in charge. Even though the other people round the table were his friends, they didn't speak unless spoken to. They waited to see what mood Frank was in. They were treading on egg shells until he dictated the mood. They were relieved that Frank seemed very relaxed. Loosened by a few slugs of Jack Daniels on the rocks, and prompted by Mike Connors, he began to reminisce about his life and career.

He told us about his childhood days of hustling on the "mean streets," making a dollar 30 cents on a Hoboken version of heads and tails, the move into show business via the Tommy Dorsey band, the ups and downs, and finally stardom and Hollywood where, thanks to that comeback of all comebacks in the film, "From Here to Eternity," he won an Oscar and became one of the biggest celebrities of all time.

This was exactly what we had hoped for. All our wish list had come true. Frank Sinatra, who hated the press, never gave interviews, was talking candidly about his career and his friends. There was so much information, how was I going to remember everything? We knew it would be too dangerous to bring in notebooks or tape recorders but I had slipped a pen into my clutch bag. I surreptitiously picked up my place card and went to the ladies. I had to pass four security guards on the way. They all nodded respectfully as I went by.

In a cubicle in the ladies I wrote brief notes in minuscule hand writing on the place card, then put it into the mirror compartment in my bag. Back past the nodding security guards, I tried not to look guilty and hoped they wouldn't ask to see inside my bag.

At the table, Frank was making sure my glass was continually topped up. We had moved on to the liqueurs and Frank recommended a favourite of his, a yellow coloured Italian liqueur, Strega. I told him I had never had it before. He urged me to give it a try. "I think you'll like it." So after loads of wine, I moved on to the Strega. How could I refuse Frank Sinatra? Every time my glass was half empty, Frank nodded to the waiter to top me up. They were only tiny glasses but there were a lot of them coming my way.

While we knocked back the liqueur, which was an incredible 40 per cent proof, Frank talked about his friends, including Humphrey Bogart, Spencer Tracy, Kirk Douglas and Robert Mitchum. He said, "Douglas and Mitchum protected me so much that I always send them a card on Mother's Day.

"They were the big guys and I was small. I remember one time in some restaurant a couple of guys came over to our table and one of them yanked me by the jacket, nearly ripping it off my shoulders. Mitchum got up and held this fellow's cheek between his finger and thumb and said to him, 'You don't want to cause any trouble now, do you?' He didn't hurt him but the guy got the message."

Every anecdote sent me to the ladies. I had soon used up all of the place card. I tried writing on toilet paper but it was taking too long and kept tearing. I flushed it down the loo. Sitting on the toilet I looked around for something to write on. It was there right in front of me: my thighs. I scribbled quote after quote above my stocking tops.

I fell into a bizarre routine: Strega, anecdote, toilet, write on thighs, Strega, anecdote, toilet, write on thighs.

The other guests probably thought I had a bladder problem. Or that I was OCD like Frank was reputed to be, apparently obsessed with showering and washing his hands.

Frank may have been 72 but he was still very sexy. He was still handsome, still desirable. It didn't matter what he said, he could have been reciting a shopping list – his voice was soft, smooth and very sensual. He was charming. He held my chair for me when I returned to the table. He laughed at the men's jokes, sent himself up and held the eyes of the ladies. When the waiter told him there was no espresso coffee, he yelled, laughing, "Close the joint! Never mind, I'll stick to this," and he raised another glass of Strega in a toast to us all.

Eventually Barbara came over to remind Frank that we should make a move to the show. "Hey I'm an usher now!" Frank declared. According to our schedule of events we were going to the Ziegfeld Room to see Donn Arden's $10m extravaganza "Jubilee." But Frank had other ideas. Into his Strega stride he asked, "Show? What show? Who wants to see the show? Come on let's have a show of hands. Why don't you stay and drink with me?"

No-one left our table. If Frank Sinatra asks you to stay and drink with him, that's what you do. The rest of the guests, including the two English women, filed out of the room to go to watch the show. We carried on drinking and I carried on Strega, anecdote, toilet, write on thighs.

Much, much later, Frank decided he would go to the casino. As we stood up, the nearest security guard talked to the radio in his sleeve, "Mr Sinatra is standing up now."

The next security guard whispered to his sleeve, "Mr Sinatra is walking away from the table." The commentary preceded us all the way: "Mr Sinatra is walking to the elevator," "Mr Sinatra is getting into the elevator." It was the sort of scenario you see in movies about the President.

Frank took my hand and put it through his arm. He held on to my hand. I noticed how soft his hands were. We strolled, arm in arm, through the hotel corridors with Ian and the rest of the guests from our table following behind. Frank said, "I love your dress. Beautiful colours." I replied that it had been a last minute buy and it was by Kanga, a friend of Prince Charles. I added, "Princess Diana has one."

Then he asked me, "Are you having a good time?"

I replied, "Amazing. Thank you. I am just a little sad that my mum will never know I have met you. She was a huge fan but she died 18 months ago."

He leaned in to whisper in my ear. I could feel his breath. He smelled sweet. A mixture of lavender water and soap. "What do you mean? Of course she knows. Your mom and my mom are up there on that hill together, babe. Right now – looking down on us."

As we entered the casino we were greeted with a crowd of fans. I was taken aback. Frank felt my arm tense in his as we entered the room. He took my hand and kissed it gently. He must have done this thousands of times but he appreciated that it was strange for me. "It's OK, babe," he whispered.

We walked slowly along the red carpet so everyone could get a good look at Frank. His visit to the casino would have been his thank you to Bally's who were sponsoring the Magic Carpet Weekend. It never did any harm to let punters know there was a mega star in the building.

'Hi Frank,' 'Frank, Frank.' The fans called. He smiled and nodded back.

'Who's that with him?' someone asked as we wandered by.

'Don't recognise her, who is it?' I heard as a Chinese whisper weaved its way through the throng. 'Who is she?'

Of course, they wouldn't recognise the young woman on Frank Sinatra's arm.

It was me. Sandra White. Former pupil of Abbey Wood Comprehensive School being held close by Frank Sinatra, melting as he whispered in my ear and hoping the notes I'd written on my thighs weren't smudging.

We arrived at an empty Black Jack table which had also been cordoned off, the croupier waiting patiently for us to arrive. The crowds were allowed to get just close enough to see that it was indeed Ol' Blue Eyes himself about to have a flutter.

Frank pulled a stool out for me to sit on and sat next to me. Bill Stapley, his English valet who had been working for him for 18 years, gave us a pile of chips. He would make sure Frank didn't go over his agreed limit of $30,000. 'I've got lady luck with me tonight,' warned Frank as he put his arm around my waist. The dinner guests who had ducked out of the show and Bobby Marx filled the remaining seats. Others stood around watching over our shoulders. Barbara arrived from the show and stood opposite us.

I confided in Frank, 'I've only seen this in the films.'

He smiled. "It's easy, babe. Easy. It's just luck. You feeling lucky? I'd gamble on rain drops running down a window pane. That's why Bill here makes sure I keep to my limit."

The croupier dealt the cards. Frank won. Then I won. I won again and again. My pile of chips was getting bigger and bigger. It was unbelievable, I didn't seem to be able to lose. Frank pulled me closer and whispered in my ear, "Shall we let someone else have a chance?" He signalled for Bill to come over and spoke quietly to him. Bill nodded that he understood and came round to my other side. Leaning closer to me so no-one else could hear, he asked, "Are you happily married?'

"What?"

"Frank wants to know if you're happily married or not," he repeated.

What a strange question. I wasn't married but I had to keep up the pretence. Why did Frank want to know if I was happily married or not? Bill spelt it out for me: "If you're happily married that's OK. But if not, Mr. Sinatra is inviting you to join him in in his suite later."

Frank Sinatra was inviting me to join him in his suite! But only if I wasn't happily married. Was I getting this right? He had asked his valet to proposition me right in front of his wife!

Now I knew that the vibes I thought I had imagined were real. Did Frank Sinatra really fancy me? I was an ordinary mum from Sevenoaks. He had had some of the most beautiful women in the world. Would he be interested in me? Mike Connors had said Frank thought I was intriguing, but even so.

41

Did I fancy him? Absolutely no doubt. He oozed sex appeal. Even though he was in his seventies, he was still a very sexy man. He even smelled sexy. He breathed sex in my ear! Besides, I was only pretending to be married. I was actually single and free to spend the night with whoever I wanted.

Did I want to spend the night with Frank? You bet, but I hesitated. Firstly I was an undercover reporter and I never mixed pleasure with my work. Secondly, my thighs were full of notes! Imagine taking my clothes off and revealing I had been writing on my legs all evening. Not a good look. I would be instantly rumbled and a definite candidate for the concrete boots.

While I was deciding what to do next, Barbara came round to Frank and kissed him on his cheek, saying she was going to bed.

I whispered to Bill, 'After Ian is asleep.'

Bill replied, 'I will tell Mr. Sinatra. I will wait for you outside your suite.'

If I hadn't had enough butterflies in my stomach to get this far, now they were going mad. Was I really going to spend the night with Ol' Blue Eyes, the legend?

Bill reported back to Frank and he looked at me and smiled. He announced to the table, "Well, that's me done. I've blown my limit. Unless Bill is going to let me have some more?"

Bill theatrically shook his head. Frank turned to his step son, Bobby Marx and said, "I guess I'd better turn in before your mom comes looking for me." He slid off his stool, took my hand, kissed it and said, ''Till later.'

I was about to leave the table also when the croupier said, "Wait, your winnings."

"My winnings?" I was astounded as he pushed towards me a pile of chips.

"Are you sure?" I asked.

Everyone laughed and Mike joked, "Take it quick before he changes his mind."

Ian changed our chips into cash. When we got back to our room he showed me the wad of money. There must have been hundreds of dollars. We threw it in the air like I had seen people do in the movies. Dollar bills fluttered down all over the room as Ian and I danced around them. We danced and hugged each other. Not because we had won at Black Jack but because we had successfully just spent the evening with Frank Sinatra and we were safely back in our room. We were elated. Our cover was still intact.

"Thank God for those two English women," said Ian, "They made us look good."

"I have to transcribe my notes,' I told Ian.

He said, "Notes? You didn't take a note book? We agreed no notebooks."

"No."

He laughed in disbelief when I told him I had been writing above my stocking tops. "I'll leave you to it. I'm going to bed." I didn't blame him. We were exhausted. Undercover work is stressful. You can't ever relax, you have to keep your wits about you all the time.

I hurriedly copied all the reminders I'd written on my legs onto a couple of sheets of hotel notepaper I found on the telephone table, adding everything else I could remember. When I'd finished, I hid my notes in the lining of my suitcase and, tiptoe-ing past Ian, stepped up to the open plan bathroom and ran the shower.

The writing on my legs was a nightmare to wash off. I had to scrub my thighs until they were red to get rid of it.

I quickly dried and dressed. I decided to wear again the dress I had worn to dinner. Frank had said many times how much he liked it. Creeping past Ian, I checked he was asleep. Treading over the money still scattered all over the floor, I opened the door to see Bill waiting for me.

FOUR

Ian was shaking me awake. "Sandra, Sandra, get up. You've got that fashion show lunch thing."

"What?"

"Lunch. Fashion show. Barbara Sinatra."

"Oh God, yes. How long have I got?"

"Half an hour."

"Oh no." I was exhausted but I had to get myself shifted. I hadn't had any sleep all night.

I consulted the schedule. The ladies were invited to "a small informal luncheon and Neiman Marcus fashion show." We would be able to meet Paul-Louis Orrier and see a preview of his fall/winter '88 collection. Dress should be casual, sporting attire or slacks. I quickly showered and, wearing a navy and cream sun dress, I stepped over the money still scattered around the floor of our suite and made my way to the Gables 6 and 7 Ballroom on the third floor of the Tracy Tower.

At the fashion show I sat next to Mary Kickerillo, wife of Vince Kickerillo, a long-time friend of Frank Sinatra. Kickerillo? It sounded dangerous. Mary, who used to sing under the name of Mary Miller, was lovely, vivacious and friendly. She didn't give me any scary moments.

All the time during the fashion show we were being told the prices of the garments and afterwards we were encouraged to buy something. All for Barbara's charity. They were incredibly expensive. It was a bit of an awkward moment. I wondered if I should buy something to keep up the pretence of being wealthy but I doubted my credit card would stand it after Selfridges. Dudley's wife Brogan Lane, was flicking through the racks of clothes next to me. She said, "Wow, these are very expensive, aren't they? I don't think

I will buy anything." I took comfort from that. If Brogan thought they were expensive and she wasn't going to buy anything, I wouldn't stick out as the only one who hadn't shelled out. We need not have worried. Mary Kickerillo bought the lot!

At lunch I sat next to Brogan who was giggly and shy. She saved her chocolate desert to take back to Dudley in their suite, "Because he couldn't come to lunch because he's a boy," she cooed.

I walked back to the elevators with Brogan when Barbara caught up with us. "Is everything alright with you?" she asked me.

"Yes. Lovely. Thank you."

"What a lovely dress."

"Thank you."

"Frank was telling me about the dress you wore last night. Princess Diana or something."

Frank had talked to Barbara about my dress! Unbelievable. I told her about the designer Kanga. She said, "I will have to check her out."

The lift door opened and Brogan and Barbara got in. I didn't move. I felt uncomfortable. I didn't think it would be a good idea to be in such a confined space with Barbara. "You coming in?" Brogan asked.

"No. I just remembered. I want to go to the casino shop."

Just as the lift doors closed, Barbara got out. Behind her back, Brogan raised her eyebrows at me.

Barbara and I walked together towards the main lobby. Suddenly she said, "Frank likes women who can hold their liquor."

"Oh."

"Yes. Where did you learn to drink like that?" Obviously my downing of bucket loads of Strega had not gone un-noticed by Barbara. I "learned to drink" night after night, lunchtime after lunchtime, drink for drink with the men in Fleet Street bars, but I couldn't tell her that. In Fleet Street you didn't get on unless you could drink. It was poor show to refuse a drink, especially if you were one of the few women working on national newspapers. You had to be one of the lads, and drink like them. I could. I could hold my booze better than a lot of the guys. But I couldn't tell Barbara where I had earned my drinking boots. I just smiled.

"I'm sorry?" I was stalling, trying to give myself time to think.

"Frank likes to drink into the night. He never goes to bed early. He's an insomniac. But he doesn't like drinking alone."

"Oh." I didn't like the way this conversation was going. I wanted the loud hotel carpet to swallow me up, but I kept telling myself: 'Keep calm. Say nothing."

Barbara went on. "Usually one of his old friends sits up drinking with him until he is ready to turn in. Apparently he had a new drinking companion last night."

I wasn't going to give anything away. "That's nice."

Then she told me how she had met Frank. She was confiding in me as if I was one of her Palm Beach girlfriends. "I was still married to Zeppo but our marriage had been over for a long time. I had all Frank's records but I did not care about knowing him because of the press I'd read. It wasn't a pretty picture."

She changed her mind when Sinatra brought his movie, 'Come Blow Your Horn' and its cast, to one of her charity evenings. She explained, "I was hit like a sledge hammer."

I thought I had better say something. "Well, it's obvious he adores you."

"Does he?"

"He said he did."

"Did he? When?"

When? Was she trying to trick me into confessing I had spent the night with her husband?

"Yes. When he was showing us around his trains, he pointed out special ones you had bought him. He said exactly that, he adored you," I replied, truthfully.

She smiled.

Quickly changing the subject, I said, "I'm going to buy my children a souvenir."

Barbara replied: "Oh yes, you have children. How many?"

"Two."

We continued our girly chat about my children as we made our way towards the shops. Then Barbara said, "Nice to talk to you Sandra. See you later. 7pm. Cocktails. Metro 1." She knew the schedule off by heart.

"Yes. Looking forward to it."

She left me. I wandered on a while longer then turned into the casino lobby. I stopped to think, leaning against a wall. I took a few deep breaths. Did that really happen? What did Barbara know? Did she really feel threatened by an ordinary mum from England? Did she really think Frank would get up to something with me? Even more importantly, did Barbara Sinatra dish out the concrete boots the same as her husband?

I looked across the room at the public phone box. I had intended to ring Bill Hagerty and my children. I looked around. I could feel eyes on me. Better not go anywhere near that phone. Instead I went to the shop and bought the children a tacky clock each. The numbers on the dial were red and black die. Ironic, really, seeing as in the casinos there is no daylight and no clocks, so the punters have no idea what time it is and carry on gambling hour after hour.

When I got back to our room, the chamber maid was picking up the money we had scattered all over the place.

"You win big!" she grinned.

The massive sunken bath looked so inviting. Ian had said he was meeting a couple of the other guests for lunch. He had taken a liking to Gene Autry and wanted to spend more time with him. So after the housekeeper left I ran myself the bubbliest, largest bath I had ever had. I leaned back in the perfumed suds. I lifted my legs and rubbed soap on my thighs where I had written notes the previous evening.

I languished in the warmth and thought back over the events of the last couple of days.

I remembered the previous evening: Bill Stapley taking me to Frank's room. I didn't think it was the suite he was sharing with Barbara. I knew from our schedule they were in Penthouse 'A' and this wasn't a penthouse. It was an open plan room like ours. Barbara wasn't in the bed! Despite Frank's womanising reputation, I didn't expect him to be entertaining me – or anyone else – in the lounge while his wife slept a few yards away.

Frank was sitting on the sofa, Jack Daniels in hand. He had discarded his tie and jacket. His shoes had been shrugged off under the coffee table. He stood up as I arrived. "Hey babe. Come in. Strega or something else?" I dare not start mixing my drinks. "Strega sounds good." Bill went to the bar in a corner of the room and poured me a LARGE Strega. He served our drinks and put the bottle and an ice bucket on the coffee table. Then he quietly left the room.

"Sit," Frank ordered, patting the sofa next to him, "Did you have a good evening?"

"It was lovely," I said honestly and nervously.

"It's good to talk about old times," said Frank, "sometimes I can't believe the life I've had.

"When you get to my age you look back a lot. You appreciate your friends, family.

"What about you? Your family?"

I told him I had two sisters and we were very close. They had been very supportive through my divorce and we were helping each other through the grief of losing our mum at the young age of 59.

He asked about my children. I told him how much I was missing them and that I had fallen in love with LA so much I was certain that if I had my children with me, I wouldn't be going back.

"Don't go back. Get them over here, babe," he urged.

"Well, it isn't that easy, they are happy in their schools, have loads of friends and there is no way I could ever move them away from their Dad."

"I can tell you love those kids. I bet they know it."

"Oh I tell them all the time."

"Yeah, kids need to know their mom loves them. I knew my mom loved me. It's the best kind of love. Women come and go, your mom is there for ever.

"If ever you decide you want to move over here. Let me know. I'll make sure everything goes OK. I'll look after you all."

Frank Sinatra would look after us all! I believed him.

I thanked him and asked if he had any plans to be in the UK soon. "You could come to my house for tea."

"Tea?" he laughed raising his glass.

"Yes. Tea and cake."

He laughed again, "Do you know what babe, I'd like that. I'm going to take you up on that. Next time I'm over there, I'm coming to your place for tea and cake."

We talked way into the night, me and Frank Sinatra, like two old friends. He said he loved my eyes. He thought my hands were "beautiful and feminine." Frank thought I was "refined" and had good manners. "English manners, you're a real English lady," he said.

I think he liked me because I was obviously besotted – hanging on to his every word at dinner. He didn't realise I was darting off every so often to write notes on my legs! But I wasn't just paying attention because I had to, he was mesmerising.

I told him Ian and I had been playing his music almost non-stop to get into the mood for the weekend and I had discovered 'The Summer Wind.'

"Yeah, I like that one." And he sang it to me. Holding me close, he sang in my ear. It was electric. Frank Sinatra singing to me – just me – my favourite Frank Sinatra song. It was seductive. Seductive.

As daylight crept into the room, Frank held me in his arms and kissed me softly on my nose and forehead. "Thank you for getting me through the night babe," he whispered, "I hate the darkness of the night. Can't bear to be alone in the dark."

Throughout the night I spent with him, I never broke my cover. I thought about it but how could I? He liked me but he hated journalists. I wasn't sure he liked me enough to overcome his hatred of journalists.

And as for his OCD: in the whole night we spent together I never saw any evidence of that.

I laid back in the bubbles and laughed out loud. Imagine a cavalcade of Frank and his entourage turning up in my cul de sac in Sevenoaks! Imagine Frank Sinatra sitting on my sofa drinking tea!

When Ian returned I was wrapped in a warm, thick fluffy white bath robe, stretched out on the bed, flicking through my photos of my children. He had found out that there would be a photographer at the evening's event. We were desperate to get some photographs of us with Frank which would be used alongside our article.

There had been a photographer at the previous evening's pre-dinner cocktails but he didn't take any of Frank. There was no way we could risk taking a camera and in any case Frank wouldn't pose unless he wanted to. Somehow we had to try to get some photos of Frank.

I dressed in a beautiful black Frank Usher midi length gown – the children's favourite. The top was a fitted bodice, with a deep V front and back, which cascaded into black lace scattered with sequins. I loved it. I added a little gold tassel necklace which I had given to my mum. Ian wore a dark suit, blue shirt and tie. We looked the part again. We braced ourselves for another round of pretence.

Our schedule told us to go to Metro 1 (26th floor) for cocktails. We mingled and made small talk with the other guests, the ladies mostly talking about the earlier fashion show. Barbara said Paul-Louis had been delighted at the outcome. I bet he was. Mary Kickerillo put her finger to her lips asking us to keep quiet. She had not told her husband Vince that she had spent a small fortune on designer clothes that afternoon.

"Won't he find out?" I asked her.

"Oh, I'll tell him when I'm good and ready. No big deal." No big deal? Spending thousands in a few minutes at a fashion show! But Vince was a very close friend of the Sinatras and helped them a lot with the Children's Centre. I expect Mary would persuade him it was OK because the proceeds were going to the Centre.

The two English women obviously spent more time in designer departments than I did. They looked my dress up and down and asked, "Frank Usher?" I nodded and they replied, "So are ours."

A photographer circulated among us taking random pics and we were delighted when Frank agreed to pose with us: we had the vital pictures for the feature.

After cocktails we were going to see the Dean Martin show and the buzz around the room was whether Frank would get up and sing. Everyone hoped to hear Frank sing at some point over the weekend. Mike Connors told us Frank rarely sang at events like this and, as for singing with Dean Martin, that would depend on what state Dean was in, whether he was sober or not. Frank called him "Drunkie."

There had been some stories in the papers that Frank and Dean had fallen out. Mike told us that Frank had insisted he would never be on the same stage as him again but he thought he was mellowing towards his old buddy. He said he was pretty certain we would not be going to the Dean Martin show if Frank didn't want to. Everyone was excitedly speculating – and hoping – that Frank could be persuaded to sing with Dean.

After an hour of cocktails we were escorted to the Celebrity Room where we were shown to front row seats around little tables. We noticed that Frank wasn't with us and the rumour started to spread that he was going to appear on stage.

The show started. Dean came out to rapturous applause, but no sign of Frank. Perhaps he was waiting in the wings ready for Dean to bring him on. Dean launched into his next number, no Frank.

Then Frank appeared alongside us and, shaking his head, took a seat in the front row. Dean had spotted him arriving and announced to the audience, "Well, look who's here. Ol' Blue Eyes himself. Come up and join me Frank." The audience went wild and a spotlight focused on Frank.

Frank looked very displeased and, smiling through gritted teeth, shook his head. He said to us, "I had decided I would sing if he was sober. I went to his dressing room before the show. I'm not singing with a drunk." That was it. Everyone was disappointed. Their chance of hearing Frank sing had gone. And all because Dean Martin had been at the booze.

I was disappointed not to hear Frank sing – again – but I closed my eyes and re-lived him singing 'The Summer Wind' just to me.

After the Dean Martin show we were taken to the Metro 2 room on the 26th Floor for dinner. Ian wondered if we would be on the same table as Frank again. "I doubt it," I said, thinking back to my earlier conversation with Barbara.

"Well it won't be those English women, they've burnt their boats."

"Yes, but there are other guests. He has got to share himself out."

We weren't on Frank's table but we were as good as. He was sitting on one table and I was sitting diagonally across from him on the adjacent table. Several times throughout dinner he caught my eye and winked.

The photographer was hovering. The two English women asked him to take their picture with Frank. He was hesitant and looked behind him to another table where Barbara was sitting. She shook her head.

Then Frank called over to me, "Hey Sandra, come here babe, let's get our photo taken." He was obviously still cross and making a point to the two English women. We went and stood by him. I bent down and whispered in his ear, "Thank you."

He took my hand, kissed it, and placed it over his shoulder. The disbelieving photographer took the snap of me holding hands with Frank Sinatra.

FIVE

The following morning, Sunday, we took the escalator to Sinatra's restaurant on the second floor of Tracy Tower for a farewell champagne brunch. Barbara and Frank circulated, thanking everyone for coming. Frank shook my hand and, holding on to it, said quietly, "Remember, I'm here. I'll look after you."

We said goodbye to Mike Connors who had spent a lot of time with us and was a really nice, down to earth guy. Dudley Moore came up to Ian and I and asked if we were going back to LA and would we like a lift. The plan had been to all travel independently – we wouldn't be in Frank's private jet, as there was no point in any of us returning to Palm Springs. We knew we wouldn't be seeing Frank again after this brunch, so we thought we may as well accept Dud's offer.

As our luggage was loaded into the limo, it made me smile when I noticed that our cases were new and expensive while millionaire Dudley and Brogan had travelled with cheap plastic hold-alls. Ian and I, still playing our parts, were in smart, expensive casual clothes. Dudley was in tatty, torn jeans, a baggy worn T shirt and flip-flops!

I was surprised when the limo took us to Las Vegas airport. In my naivety I had thought that when Dudley offered us a lift, he meant a lift in his car to LA. What he actually meant was a lift from Las Vegas to LA in his private Lear Jet!

Ian and I sat opposite Dudley and Brogan in the tiny cabin. An air stewardess served us drinks and gave Brogan a sick bag! While we sipped on our beers, Brogan threw up into the bag. Dudley explained, "She suffers from air sickness, take-off and landing. She'll be alright in a minute."

The flight was just over an hour long, just enough time for us all to digest the weekend. We all agreed it had been an amazing experience but it was a shame Frank didn't sing. I couldn't tell them he did sing – to me, in the middle of the night.

When we landed and our bags were unloaded onto the tarmac, we said our goodbyes and went our separate ways. Ian and I calmly walked through the airport to get to our waiting limo – Ian still insisting we should keep up the pretence. Even in the limo we didn't give anything away. The sliding doors between us and the driver were closed but we weren't going to take any chances.

On the way back to Santa Monica we asked the driver to pull over at a local store where we stocked up on some groceries and a bottle of champagne.

It wasn't until we were safely back inside Jeff Bridges' house, with our bags dumped in the middle of the living room, that we allowed ourselves to really let go. We danced around the living room, proud of ourselves.

Ian admitted, "I was never sure we would pull that off."

I agreed, "There were a couple of hairy moments but we did it!"

I couldn't wait to ring the office to tell them we had done it. I called Bill. "We're back home now."

"How was it?"

"We did it. Amazing."

"Well done Sandra. I can't wait to read about it. When can I expect copy?"

"Tomorrow. I'll write it in the morning."

I rang my children and told them I was back from my weekend with Frank Sinatra and that I had found a fun present for them.

The phone went non-stop with Ian's friends, including Jeff Bridges, checking that we were back safe and sound. They were genuinely afraid for us. They didn't know what would happen to us if we had been rumbled, but they knew it would have been bad news. Ian told them all about the two women from North London who unwittingly had taken the heat off us.

The next morning Ian set up his portable typewriter on the dining room table which divided the kitchen from the living room. We laid out all the information we had collected: the schedule, a leaflet about Bally's, the welcome letter from Barbara and Frank, and we set to revealing the secrets of our weekend.

I had already written it in my head. I have been a journalist since I was 18. Writing and intros come naturally to me. The whole feature had been buzzing around in my head all weekend. I was desperate to get it down on paper.

The editor had decided that the article should be a two-parter and that the first part would launch the new Sunday Mirror colour supplement. I wrote what amounted to a tribute to Frank, almost an open fan letter. It was a totally accurate account of our weekend with him. He had been charming, good fun, welcoming, a pleasure to be with. I was proud of the feature and I was delighted it was going to appear in our new colour supplement. I decided I would send Frank a copy. I was still a bit nervous about the concrete boots but I thought Frank would have found our escapade amusing and I know he would not have had any complaints about what I had written.

I filed the piece to our copy takers in London – the people who type out your story while you dictate it over the phone. Reporters rarely get to meet these men and women but over many times of filing in copy, you get to know each other. Nothing fazes them: they have typed out stories ranging from the horrific to the ridiculous, but the story of my undercover weekend with Frank Sinatra had them enthralled right from the start.

Instead of the usual monotone, "Yes. Yes," as they encouraged you to continue, they were asking, "What? You actually went into his home? What was it like?"

"I'm getting to that," I would reply.

When I finished, I said to Ian, "Well, the copy takers liked it, that's a good sign." It was. Copy takers weren't backwards in coming forwards with their opinions on what you were filing. An award winning sports writer once told me a copy taker had complained, "I hate football. Why can't you write about flowers?"

Fortunately for us, copy takers weren't the only ones who liked our piece. Bill rang and passed on the editor's compliments. "This is a fantastic read, Sandra. Go to the best restaurant and have a bloody good lunch. You deserve it. But first what about pics?"

I told Bill the only pics we had were the ones taken by the Sinatra's nervous snapper. We had been promised they would be sent to us soon.

Ian rang Barbara's staff and, turning on the Sean Connery charm again, asked if the photographs could be couriered to us rather than posted. He said I would soon be returning to the UK and wanted to take them with me to show my children. They agreed. We received a letter from Barbara, thanking us for going, saying they had enjoyed having us with them and promising to send on the photos as soon as they were ready.

Taking Bill up on his offer, the next day we headed off into LA for a fabulous lunch at another celebrity restaurant. Joan Collins was a few tables away. We spent all afternoon getting absolutely hammered.

Ian's friends wanted to hear all about our adventure so we found ourselves constantly being invited out. They all treated us like heroes: they couldn't believe we had managed to fool Sinatra and his massive security operation. Jeff Bridges invited us to the private screening for his family of his latest move, 'Tucker: The Man and His Dream.'

We met up with his sister Cindy, who was also a close friend of Ian, and some Bridges' family friends for a hamburger before going to the small screening cinema in Hollywood. Cindy and I immediately hit it off. She was homely and good fun. At the screening you would have thought Ian and I were the stars. Jeff wanted everyone to know what we had been up to. He introduced me all the time like, "This is Sandra, she has just spent the weekend with Frank Sinatra," then, of course, everyone would want to hear all about it. Even in Hollywood, his home town, Frank had become an enigma. Hollywood is full of legends, but none, it seemed, as big as Frank Sinatra.

As the lights went down and the film began, I had to pinch myself that I was in an intimate cinema watching Jeff Bridges' as yet unreleased movie WITH Jeff and his family and close friends.

'Tucker' tells the story of Preston Tucker and his attempts to market the 1948 Tucker Sedan against opposition from the car manufacturing giants of the time. As we filed out, we all congratulated Jeff but I thought we were all a bit subdued. I couldn't have been the only one who thought Jeff had made a big mistake. It was dreadful. He played Preston Tucker almost like a larger than life caricature. I thought he over-acted throughout. But that wouldn't have been his fault. Some of Jeff's friends said he only did the film because he wanted to work with the director, Francis Ford Coppola. Jeff obviously trusted Coppola and went with him. But the family and friends who filed out weren't the excited, animated throng who went in.

Every day the office was putting pressure on me about the pictures. Every day Ian rang Barbara's office but there wasn't much else we could do. They were beginning to get impatient with Ian and told him they would send them as soon as they had them. We even rang Bally's to try to get hold of the photographer to ask him direct to get a move on but we didn't have any luck there either. We just had to sit and wait. I was as impatient as everyone else. I knew the office wouldn't pull me out until the job was complete – the minute they had those pics I would be going home. I was still madly in love with Jeff's house and LA but I missed my children. And they were missing me. Every phone call now started with, "When are you coming home, mum?" It tugged at my heart strings.

Cindy Bridges invited us down to the family's beach house at Malibu. From the outside it was just an ageing grey fence on the main Pacific Coast Highway. All the houses were hidden from the road by high fences. Their neighbours included Barbra Streisand. Beyond the fence was a small, cosy wooden house right on the beach. Cindy told me her parents had owned it for years and she and her brothers, Jeff and Beau, who was also an actor, had spent very many happy hours there. Cindy's husband was there and a friend of his who worked for the Disney Corporation designing new rides for

Disney World. He was fascinated with rockets and disappeared into the sand dunes to set off a rocket while we watched from the veranda. The rocket wasn't an everyday firework, it was a large heavy duty contraption which took a lot of setting up and caused a massive explosion when it took off. It impressed the guys, us girls couldn't see the attraction.

Ian took me sightseeing to Venice Beach. Everyone seems to be on wheels in Venice Beach – bikes, roller skates or skateboards. And, of course the shops are filled with the same. I spotted the ideal present for the children: skateboards decorated with the Stars and Stripes. I bought two without even thinking how I would get them home.

I went into an art gallery and recognised a piece of art work. I knew I had seen it before I just couldn't remember where. I wracked my brains and eventually realised it had been on the wall by the ladies toilet in the restaurant where Ian and I had got drunk celebrating our Sinatra success. It was 'You are Going on a Trip,' an etching by Charles Garabedian. I had stopped to admire it on several trips to the ladies. I thought it would be a perfect souvenir – I was on an incredible trip - so I bought it and arranged to have it shipped back to Sevenoaks.

We met up with Dan and Darling McVicar a few times and had a boozy night out with some other friends of Ian who sang in a choir, during which a poet nicked my poem. I often write poetry just for myself when I have been moved by certain events. Apart from having a couple published when I was very young, no-one ever sees them. I had loved Jeff's house so much I wrote a poem about the way it made me feel. I called it 2882 Hume Road. One of the men at dinner told us he was a poet. Apparently he had released a few LP's of poems. Tipsy, I told the table I had written a poem on this trip. "Let's hear it," they all urged. So I recited my poem for my new friends.

Malibu mist curls around its secrets as I lay beside mine

Haze hides endless faults as I ponder ours

I am an empty coat hanger waiting for you to take off your jacket

Yet the chill lingers

A pink moon hugs the horizon, calling me

I may return

When you are warm.

Graciously, everyone applauded and said it was lovely. Shortly afterwards I went to the ladies and when I tried to get out the big, burly poet was blocking my way. "Hey," he said, "your poem was cool, say it again." Obligingly I recited it again. "Slower," said the poet. I realised he was writing down MY poem! It was a few days later when it dawned on me my poem might be heading for an LP.

Something I ate that night made me very ill. I blamed the clams. I struggled through 24, 48 hours of sickness thinking it would be over soon. I was taking various medications Ian recommended but nothing was working. Ian was worried about me and took me to see a doctor. He said if I didn't improve in 24 hours I would have to go into hospital. No way. I told Ian I couldn't go into hospital, I needed to get home. We still hadn't received the photographs from the Magic Carpet Weekend people but when we did, I wanted to go home. The longer I was ill, the more I wanted to go home.

My boss, no doubt getting increasingly fed up that I was still in LA for the features department, started coming up with other stories for me to cover while I was there. I had to doorstep Princess Stephanie of Monaco in 90°F. And while I was still ill I kept an appointment to see the lawyer of Samantha Geimer, the girl Roman Polanski drugged and raped when she was 13. I asked him if I could have an interview with her. He said he would let me know but I didn't hold out much hope. Amazingly a few days later he called to say she would see me and I had the first ever exclusive interview with her when she described Polanski plying her with champagne, taking pictures of her in a Jacuzzi before sexually assaulting her and giving her a sleeping pill. It was a major coup for our paper. My boss was happy. My colleagues, seeing my name in the paper at last, thought Samantha was the special I was on. My weekend with Frank still hadn't made the paper because we were still waiting on the photographs. So I carried on doing news stories, including interviewing the newly estranged husband of a soap star.

The editor was getting impatient and thinking about running the piece without the photographs, using stock pics of Frank. Bill was trying to persuade her to wait. Fortunately, before she could do that a courier arrived out of the blue with a package from Barbara's office. Ian and I excitedly spread the photos out on the kitchen table. It made the whole thing seem even more surreal, opening the envelope to see photographs in red velvet frames of me with Frank, holding hands, smiling at the camera. Ian immediately organised another courier to take them to London, along with the other documents we had saved from the weekend.

Once the package of pics arrived in London, I expected to be pulled out so Ian invited a few friends round for a little farewell party for me. I insisted he kept all of the wine glasses the Sinatra's had given us. It was unlikely they would survive the journey back to the UK. On a shopping trip to Rodeo Drive I bought him some gold cuff links as a thank you for looking after me. And, using my 'winnings' from the Black Jack table, I treated myself to a beautiful Art Deco diamond brooch. I told everyone Frank Sinatra had bought it for me!

Eventually, four weeks after I had arrived in LA for a ten day job, I found myself back at the airport. Ian dropped me off, we hugged goodbye and, with some sadness, I watched his little red Mazda disappear. It's a rule that reporters have to ring the desk before they get on any plane, so just before I checked in my luggage I found a pay phone and called the office. I expected them to say, "All good Sandra. See you when you get back." But the news editor said, "Don't get that flight. Get the first flight to Vancouver."

"Vancouver?"

I looked at the skateboards and cried. I was being sent on another major story. It was six weeks before I got home.

During that time the supplement came out with a specially commissioned art work of Frank on the cover with the headline 'Come Fly With Me.' It was a re-working of the cover for his 1958 album, 'Come Fly With Me.' It wouldn't have taken much research by the art department to discover Sinatra hated it, saying it looked like an advertisement for the TWA airline. Despite that, the magazine cover looked stunning and the Frank Sinatra story was picked up throughout the world. The sub editors had not interfered with my words, it went in as I had written it, under the headline, 'Sinatra: The Man and His Musings.' They also used the photo of me and Ian with Frank, a library picture of Dudley with Brogan, an aerial pic of The Compound, some library shots of Frank on stage and … a picture taken without Frank knowing of him relaxing on a sun lounger in his Palm Springs garden. It wasn't an exclusive new pic. It had recently emerged and had been used in the papers who had described him as over the hill and podgy. It wasn't flattering. The way he was sitting made him look as though he had a bulging beer belly. Frank was obviously not as lean as he was in his younger days, but I had not seen any evidence of him being flabby when we were in Las Vegas. I couldn't understand why the editor chose to use a pic that made him look a has been when the whole piece was about him being charming, sexy, still a star.

I am sure the article was seen by Frank's people and I'm certain none of them would have been able to look beyond the awful photograph across the top of the page. It didn't matter that the text was favourable, the photograph was horrid. There was no way I could send him the magazine. Ian and I were beside ourselves with disappointment that everything we had been through seemed to have been ruined by using that grubby pic.

It wasn't until two months after my undercover weekend that I eventually made it back to the office. I discovered that, even after that time, everyone was still talking about it. I was congratulated by my bosses and my colleagues. Friends, colleagues and even reporters from opposition newspapers took me for lunch and drinks to hear all about it. I even got offered a job on a rival newspaper.

I have often wondered what Frank Sinatra thought when he was told about our undercover sting. After all, it made the two English women swapping the place cards look a bit tame! I resigned myself to the fact that Frank Sinatra wouldn't be driving down my cul de sac in Sevenoaks and coming in for tea.

So far I have avoided the concrete boots.

EPILOGUE

Frank Sinatra died on May 14th, 1998, aged 82.

I believe Jeff Bridges' beautiful house was lost in the earthquake of 1994.

The Compound was sold to a Canadian entrepreneur in 1995 and is used for corporate functions. The sale included Frank's grand piano, all his memorabilia, his paintings and even his trains.

Dan McVicar, now a producer, writer and director in Hollywood and Europe, has clocked up over 550 episodes with The Bold and the Beautiful.

My sisters and I wore the glamorous gowns many times before I donated them to a charity shop.

My children loved the skate boards. Shortly after this trip I resigned so I could spend more time with them.

I have been photographed with many famous people but I'm not one of those journalists who displays them about the place. There is only one on my sideboard: me and Frank Sinatra.

ACKNOWLEDGEMENTS

I am incredibly grateful to Mel and Sam who helped me in so many ways. I also want to thank Frank Thorne and Peter Dyke for their enthusiasm and encouragement. Massive thanks to my loyal gang of supporters, led by Frances and Christine.

Sandra White is a journalist and writer. In Fleet Street she worked in news, features, crime and showbiz before editing a high profile magazine. She has recently returned from Australia where she spent ten years covering Australia and South East Asia for British national newspapers. She has also written for TV and film. She is now working on a crime novel and a TV series. She lives in Kent and Spain.

Follow me on Twitter @WriterSandra

www.facebook.com/SandraWhiteWriter

www.sandrawhite.co.uk

Sandra White is now working on a crime novel based on her experience as a crime reporter in Fleet Street.

LITTLE PLUMS is the first in the Helen Ross series.

Here is an exclusive preview.

LITTLE PLUMS

CHAPTER ONE

I am going to kill my boss. I've written a list of what I need: one of those paper suits forensic guys wear, complete with mask, gloves and shoe coverings. And a gun, of course. A gun with a silencer. Then, when he's working late alone in the office, I'll walk in, shoot him and leg it. I'll have to burn everything I'm wearing and chuck the gun in the Thames. That's about as near perfect a murder you can get, according to JJ.

He should know, he's a cop.

Actually, a former cop. He spectacularly goes from B.E.M. to bent before he is 40. Exposed during the biggest investigation into police corruption the country has ever seen, he miraculously escapes prison but loses his job. Now he makes a living selling to crime reporters information passed on to him by other bent coppers. His friends in the force will access files and computers for a nice cash backhander. He is my best contact. JJ is about to grab his drink. I stop him with my hand on his ancient weathered Barber and stare straight into his unusually blue eyes. 'Can you get me a gun?' I ask.

Nothing fazes JJ. He earned his medal disarming a robber who had already shot dead two cops at point blank range, but his ruddy, fresh air complexion becomes a bit redder as he replies, 'Of course I can. But for Christ's sake Ross, we all know Millen is a jam roll but why do you need to kill him? Why don't you just shoot him in the Niagara Falls?' He gives me one of his beaming smiles as he pours me a glass of champagne and asks needlessly, 'Bad day?'

Unbuttoning my suit jacket, I dissolve into the trendy little bucket chair. The champagne is bitingly cold and I let the bubbles hit my frown before I burst out, 'Millen is such a shit. I've had six consecutive splashes but he forgets that. All I get from him is a load

73

of bollocks because I haven't had a front page in a couple of weeks. There are reporters in there who haven't had their name in the paper in months but he picks on me.

'I hate Millen. I hate his weedy moustache. I hate his spindly fingers and I hate the way I can feel his eyes on my bum as I walk around the office.

'I want him dead. I want to say "take that, you bastard" and watch him squirm.'

I finish my rant but JJ says nothing. 'Well, say something then,' I prompt.

JJ doesn't come forward with the cheery comments I want. 'Come on, JJ. The reason I flogged out here was so you could cheer me up. And give me a story of course.' He is too quiet. He starts to look uncomfortable and would writhe in his seat if the velvet bucket chair wasn't grabbing his bum like a vice.

'For fuck's sake, say something,' I repeat, then I twig. 'What? What do you know?'

Because he deals with all the papers, JJ often picks up juicy gossip from the other offices which he isn't averse to passing on.

He has the decency to look sympathetic as he passes on a very worrying rumour, 'I heard Millen had lunch with the News of the World's crime guy, sounding him out, asking him if he'd consider a move from Wapping.'

'Oh that's fucking charming. I'm the Herald's crime reporter and my boss is out looking for my replacement.'

'Well, so what? Ross you're good. You're the only woman crime reporter in Fleet Street. You will soon get another job.'

'I don't want another job. I hate Millen but I love my job. I don't just love it, I need it. Shit. Shit. Shit. I need a story, have you got anything?'

He shakes his head. 'Ross if I did, I'd let you have it. I'll have a sniff around.'

On the basis of that promise I go to the bar for another bottle of Moet. JJ sells stuff to all the papers and I try to make myself top of his list by being his friend and spoiling him. Your contacts don't just want money, they need to feel important too. I have mastered the technique of filling someone with booze while I only give the impression I am putting away equal amounts. JJ often lets slip a great story after a few bevvies and if he has one in him tonight, I am determined to get it. I'm elbowing my way through the designer suited after work throng lining the bar when he puts his hand on my shoulder, 'Better get another glass. The jam roll's turned up.'

I look beyond him to see Millen hovering at our table. 'Shit. What's he doing here?' I chose to meet JJ in a trendy wine bar a couple of blocks from the office because everyone from work usually just falls down the stairs into the drinking club, The Olive, opposite.

'Looking for you. I couldn't lie. He saw your jacket on the back of the chair.'

'Oh shit. Well at least he can see I'm working.'

JJ's face crumples into mock pain, 'You mean you're only spending time with me to get a story. I thought you enjoyed my company.' I ignore him. I do enjoy his company – to a point. But I am only here to find out if he has anything. I would rather be at home, curled up on the sofa in my pyjamas watching a silly chick flick.

The wine bar is crowded but my news editor somehow manages to purloin himself a chair and drags it up to our corner table. I haven't even sat down myself before he demands, 'What are we going to do Ross?'

'About what?'

'About what? A splash, of course.'

'But it's only Tuesday,' I say feebly. As a Sunday paper, Tuesday is our first working day of the week which we usually spend doing our expenses and socialising. We don't start worrying about a front page until Thursday.

Millen takes a gulp of champagne and pulls a face, he prefers Scotch but drinks anything as long as he doesn't have to pay for it. 'Helen,' he begins. I know then this is not an ordinary idle chat after work. He hasn't found me just to be sociable. No-one in the office calls me by my first name. It's always Ross. Millen calls me Helen only when he is praising or bollocking me. Obviously I'm not expecting praise. He goes on, 'You must have something. You're the best man I've got, especially as Steve is out of it, the bastard.'

'How is he?'

'Dried out, he'll be in this week.'

'Well then....'

Millen splutters, my champagne making the moustache I hate sparkle, 'He'll be no good. He's done for and you know it. Dry out, get pissed, dry out. We'll be getting arseholed at his wake before the years out.' It hurts to hear Millen talk this way about Steve, he is a nice guy and a Herald man through and through. He is a good operator – when he's sober – so I suggest, 'Put him on with me for a while. In the old days....'

'Yeah, yeah in the old days Fleet Street looked after its alcoholics. Heard it all before Ross. We made him an alkie so we should look after him. We are. We're drying the bastard out again. Forget him. There's other things to worry about. Have you got anything?'

'I'm working on a couple of leads,' I lie, looking across to JJ who nods encouragingly, and very kindly mumbles something about if he has anything I will be the first to get it, but Millen isn't listening. He's been keeping his eye on Sky News on the huge TV at the side of the bar. You can't hear it above the chatter of the bullshitting masses but subtitles flash across the bottom of the screen. A pale faced Government Minister is being interviewed standing next to his bird like wife at the five bar gate of their country home about his new Kids Charter. Their three children play self-consciously in the background.

'Children have rights too', declares the Minister, 'they have the right to a decent education, a proper home and people to care about their well-being.' Why he has suddenly decided now is the time to start spouting off about kids' rights is anybody's guess but on a quiet news day he finds himself smugly topping the bulletins.

'That's it,' declares Millen, rubbing his long, thin hands together, 'We must have something on this Kids Charter. Helen, get to this prick and talk to him about his family. See if you can dig up some dirt.'

'I'm crime,' I protest.

'This will get your name in the paper,' he retaliates spitefully. The old adage that you are only as good as your last by-line weighs heavily on my shoulders. And, just to rub it in, he adds, 'Helen, the Herald won't carry anyone, you know that. Not Steve, not you, no-one. There are plenty of good people out there.' I exchange a knowing look with JJ who is beginning to wish he hadn't told me about Millen's lunch with the Screws guy.

I start to say the Herald doesn't carry me, I pull my weight more than most but he looks straight through me.

Bored with us now, Millen stands up – over six feet tall, thin and as cold and greasy as a rasher of streaky bacon straight from the fridge. As he turns round to retrieve his jacket, JJ pretends to shoot him and whispers, 'Take that, jam roll,' which makes me giggle. Catching me laughing, my boss instantly becomes angry. He does a hairpin bend over me. His face is so close to mine I can feel his glistening moustache twitch.

'Get a splash Helen, or look for another job.'